TOGETHER WE CAN

A STUDIO PRESS BOOK

First published in the UK in 2022 by Studio Press,
an imprint of Bonnier Books UK,
4th Floor, Victoria House, Bloomsbury Square, London WC1B 4DA
Owned by Bonnier Books,
Sveavägen 56, Stockholm, Sweden

www.bonnierbooks.co.uk

1 3 5 7 9 10 8 6 4 2

Written by Ned Hartley
Illustrated by Studio Muti
Edited by Ellie Rose
Designed by Rob Ward
Production by Emma Kidd

Special thanks to Ayoola Solarin for editorial consultation

A CIP catalogue for this book is available from the British Library
Printed and bound in China

TOGETHER
WE
CAN

WRITTEN BY
NED HARTLEY

ILLUSTRATED
BY **MUTI**

40
**INSPIRATIONAL STORIES
ABOUT WHAT HUMANS
CAN ACHIEVE WHEN
WE WORK AS A TEAM**

STUDIO PRESS

CONTENTS

INTRODUCTION

Which inventions have changed your life? What's your favourite song or piece of music? What sporting event will you never forget? What scientific discovery has changed the way that you think about the world or the universe? Every single thing that you are thinking of was achieved by a team, by individuals who understood that only by working together can we unleash incredible things.

Some books show the past as a long succession of important people who managed to achieve things because they had such powerful personalities. But we all know that life is a little bit more complicated than that, so this book is a little different. It's almost impossible to change the world on your own - the way to make a difference is to bring together brilliant people who all want the same thing.

This book is about the amazing, wonderful, inspirational and world-changing things that we can achieve when we work together. In these pages you'll see that mankind's greatest accomplishments have come from teams working to a common purpose. Humans have peered into the secrets hidden in our genetic blueprint, and taken our first incredible steps into space itself, and the only way that we have been able to do this is when we combine to become more than the sum of our parts.

From sports teams to pop groups, working together as a team is the most important thing in the world. The most exciting plays, the most beautiful songs and the greatest sporting records don't happen because of a single person, but only come from dedicated teams of

people with different skills and abilities who understand how to work together.

Ground-breaking inventions and discoveries are important, but this book also shows how much we can help each other when we come together. We can only accomplish essential achievements like environmental sustainability, political equality and animal welfare when we combine to form powerful coalitions.

This book is about the power of partnerships and collaboration, but it's also about the importance of human connection. It's about the relationships, support, strength and motivation that come from being part of a team. We can achieve a lot on our own, but together we can achieve so much more!

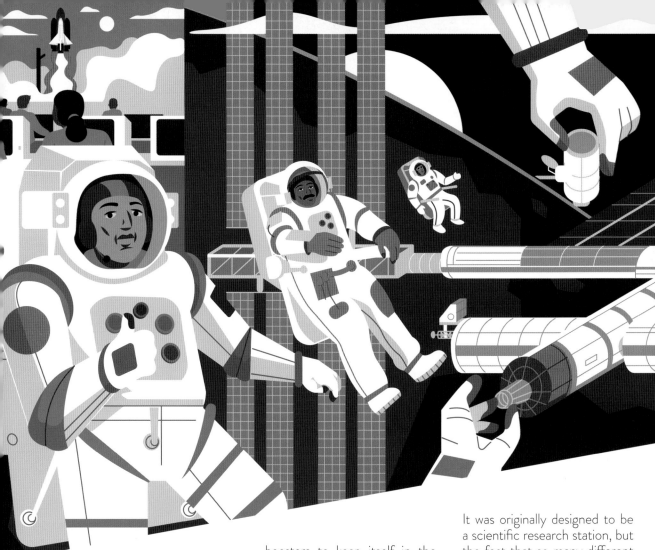

The International Space Station (ISS) is a brilliant example of how different countries can work together to create something that none could create on its own. The ISS is orbiting the Earth right now, and if you look up on the right night you might even be able to see it moving quickly across the sky like a bright star! It circles the Earth with an average height of 400 km (250 miles) and uses boosters to keep itself in the right place.

The International Space Station was first launched in November 1998 and is a collaboration between five different space agencies from Russia, the US, Europe, Japan and Canada. The space station is modular, which means that different parts can be added or removed as needed, so it is always being upgraded with new research pods, equipment and facilities.

It was originally designed to be a scientific research station, but the fact that so many different countries have sent astronauts to the ISS has been important for international relations. It has also helped people all over the world learn about space and how countries can work together on scientific research.

243 astronauts from 19 different countries (and counting) have visited the space station, and it has a regular crew of six people. It's hard living in space – space station crew have to do two

THE INTERNATIONAL SPACE STATION

hours of exercise every day or their muscles and bones start to weaken. It's a huge achievement to keep human beings alive in space, and it requires a really big team of scientists and engineers on the ground. The ground team work around the clock to make sure that astronauts have the heat, oxygen and food they need to survive.

Many important scientific and medical discoveries have been made aboard the ISS. It holds a huge device that could not easily be housed on Earth, called the Alpha Magnetic Spectrometer, which was able to detect evidence of dark matter. Dark matter is a substance that makes up a lot of our universe, but is very hard to detect (see page 18). Medical studies have shown that bacteria from Earth can survive in the harsh environment of space around the ISS, which may give some clues as to how life spreads around the universe on comets and meteorites.

The International Space Station has been described as the most expensive single thing ever constructed, and as of 2010 the total cost was estimated to be $150,000,000,000 ($150 billion!). The greatest achievement of the ISS is not a technological one, but a human one. An international partnership of space agencies has brought together astronauts, flight crews, researchers, scientists, engineers, communications crews and many more. Everyone involved is working together to expand mankind's scientific knowledge and to help each other unlock the secrets of space and the universe.

CERN AND THE LARGE HADRON COLLIDER

CERN (Conseil Européen pour la Recherche Nucléaire) is the European Organisation for Nuclear Research. It is an international scientific research organisation for the study of high-energy particle physics. There is a huge CERN laboratory on the border between France and Switzerland which brings thousands of scientists from all over the world together to collaborate on groundbreaking scientific research. Over 12,500 scientists of more than 110 nationalities collaborate at CERN.

CERN promotes the Open Science movement, which aims to make scientific research accessible to everyone. This means that all publications by CERN authors can be accessed by anyone, and the data and software are also available. Sharing research means that scientists all around the world can collaborate and build on each other's work.

CERN is the home of the Large Hadron Collider, which is the largest and most powerful particle accelerator in the world. It cost around $10 billion to create. It is a 27-km (17-mile) ring of superconducting magnets,

which is big enough to circle the entire city of Geneva. It works by creating two beams of energy, then firing them at each other at nearly the speed of light. When the beams hit each other, tiny subatomic particles smash into each other and break apart, which gives scientists a glimpse of the building blocks of creation. It's incredibly difficult work, as the particles involved are so small. It's the equivalent of firing two needles 10 km (6 miles) away from each other and making them hit in the middle. The Large Hadron Collider has a special cryogenic cooling system to keep it at -271.3°C (-456.34°F), which

means that it is colder than outer space.

The Large Hadron Collider was able to confirm the existence of the Higgs boson. The Higgs boson is a fundamental particle associated with the Higgs field, which gives mass to other particles. The Large Hadron Collider is the only place in the world where Higgs bosons can be studied. Previously, scientists had predicted the existence of these particles, but we did not have the equipment to study them. It's a very important piece of scientific discovery and helps us understand not only the past, but also the future of our

universe. Hundreds of scientists, engineers and programmers worked together on the Large Hadron Collider to make this scientific feat possible.

While it is one of the most important pieces of scientific research to have ever been attempted, the Large Hadron Collider is still at the mercy of outside influences. Animals have managed to damage the Collider twice. In 2016 a weasel chewed through electrical wiring which meant the power had to stop, and there was another power outage in 2009 when a bird dropped a bit of baguette onto electrical equipment!

SCIENCE
APOLLO 11

In 1961 President Kennedy promised to put a man on the moon within 10 years. On 20 July 1969 the first man walked on the Moon. *Apollo 11* was the eleventh mission in the Project Apollo programme, an American project where the US raced against the Soviet Union to be the first country to send a man to the Moon.

While Neil Armstrong and Buzz Aldrin were the first men to walk on the Moon's surface, it took hundreds of thousands of people to achieve such a bold and ambitious mission. Pilot Michael Collins stayed in the Command Module and did not walk on the moon's surface. *Apollo 11* had a full backup crew of astronauts who trained in simulators with the main crew and were ready to take over in case of emergency, but did not go into space. Back on Earth, there was a full support crew whose job it was to make sure that both the main and backup crews had everything they needed and were able to react to any situation.

The technology used to launch the Moon landings is very primitive by today's standards – an iPhone has over 100,000 times more processing power than the *Apollo 11* computers! The Moon landing was controlled by the Apollo Guidance Computer, which was one of the most sophisticated computers ever built at the time. It took years to build and required thousands of lines of computer code instructions to tell it what to do. Programmer Margaret Hamilton led the team that wrote the code, and there was so much that when the code was printed out, it was taller than she was.

Teams of mathematicians

$$m = \frac{AP^{*}_{t}}{\sqrt{T_{r}}} \sqrt{\frac{y}{R}} \left(\frac{y+1}{2}\right)^{\frac{-y+1}{2(y-1)}} \qquad \frac{A_{e}}{A^{*}} = \left(\frac{y+1}{2}\right) \qquad \frac{A_{P+}}{T_{t}}$$

$$\frac{T_{c}}{T_{t}} = \left(1 + \frac{y-1}{2} M_{e}^{2}\right)^{-1} \qquad M_{e}^{2})^{\frac{-y}{y-1}} \qquad \sqrt{\frac{y}{R}}^{2} \qquad \left(1 + \frac{y-1}{2}\right)$$

worked to calculate the trajectories and forces that would be needed to land on the Moon and then take off again. Dorothy Vaughn was the first Black supervisor, and one of the few female supervisors, of the team of mathematicians. If any of their calculations had been incorrect then the space mission would have failed.

Every part of the Moon landing was coordinated by a team in Mission Control on Earth. One of the most important jobs in the *Apollo 11* mission was the Capsule Communicator (also known as CapCom). This was the only person on Earth who talked directly to the flight crew, and had to clearly communicate information from the ground team at NASA – this person was always an astronaut themselves. Each of these CapComs went through the same training as the astronauts who walked on the Moon and had to know everything about the mission.

Gene Kranz was the Flight Director when *Apollo 11* landed on the Moon, which meant that he was responsible for planning the mission and managing the team in Mission Control. At its peak, the Apollo programme employed 400,000 people, each of whom contributed to one of mankind's most incredible achievements.

THE DISCOVERY OF THE NATURE OF DNA

DNA (Deoxyribonucleic acid) is the blueprint for life. Each DNA molecule is made up of two chains of atoms that coil around each other in a twisty double helix formation. These chains carry the genetic instruction for building any living organism. Everyone's DNA is different, and it tells the cells that make up their body to grow in a certain way. Everything about you, from your eye colour to your shoe size, is written in your DNA. The elegantly simple structure of the double helix eluded scientists for years – they knew that the different building blocks had to fit together, but they did not know how.

In 1950 Rosalind Franklin started working at King's College Cambridge, UK, researching the structure of DNA. Rosalind was a brilliant scientist who had perfected the art of X-ray crystallography, where X-ray beams are used to create a photograph of the structure of crystals. Despite being very talented, Rosalind found it hard at King's College, perhaps because some of the male scientists did not think that a woman should be studying such important things.

Rosalind's colleague, Maurice Wilkins, showed some of Rosalind's work to his friend Francis Crick, who was also studying the structure of DNA. Part of the work that Francis saw was a photo labelled 'Photo 51' which showed a very clear pattern in a DNA molecule. The photo had been taken by Raymond Gosling, a graduate student who was working for Rosalind. As soon as he saw the photo, Francis became very excited – he and his friend James Watson had been unable to find the structure of DNA on their own.

Francis and James worked to create a model of DNA, which showed how the different acids that make up DNA wind around each other in a double helix. When they finished their model, Francis was so excited that he stood up in his local pub in Cambridge and shouted to everyone that he had discovered 'the secret of life'. Once they had presented their findings, Maurice, Francis and James were given the Nobel Prize in Physiology or Medicine in 1962. Rosalind died in 1958, and as Nobel Prizes are only given to living people, was not eligible for the prize.

This discovery ushered in a new era of how we think about DNA and paved the way for works like the Human Genome Project (see page 30). It also allows us to study how diseases spread, and why some people are more susceptible to diseases than others.

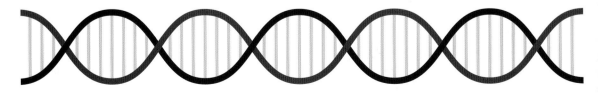

Franklin &
Gosling

DARK MATTER

How can you find something that you can't see? About 80 percent of the universe is made up of dark matter, a substance that scientists cannot directly observe because it does not emit light or energy. So how did scientists discover the evidence for dark matter? By working together.

The concept of dark matter had been discussed by scientists since the 1920s, but in the 1970s Vera Rubin and Kent Ford provided evidence that had never been seen before. Vera had always loved the stars and had stared at the night sky through a telescope from an early age. Despite not being able to get into Princeton University because they didn't accept women, she studied at American colleges, Cornell and Georgetown University.

Vera took a job as a researcher and, with fellow astronomer Kent, she studied how light changes as it comes from different places in galaxies that are shaped like a spiral. Kent had developed a spectrometer which could measure extremely faint light coming from galaxies thousands of light years away. In a spiral galaxy, stars orbit around the centre of the galaxy, so Vera and Kent expected the stars on the edge of the galaxy to move more slowly than the stars nearer the middle. This is the same way that planets at the edge of our solar system orbit more slowly than those closer to the Sun. However, this wasn't true. For the stars at the edge of the galaxy to be moving at these speeds, there had to be something with enough mass to create gravity. But it also had to be something that couldn't be seen. That something was dark matter.

Vera and Kent's work showed that the galaxies they were studying must contain about ten times as much dark matter as normal matter, but at first many astronomers did not want to accept their work. However, after further study and discussion, their work has since been confirmed and has become accepted as part of how we understand the universe. Vera was awarded the National Medal of Science and had the National Science Foundation Vera C. Rubin Observatory in Chile built in her name.

Other scientific teams have taken Vera and Kent's work even further – one team even discovered a galaxy composed almost entirely of dark matter. Called Dragonfly 44, this galaxy is as big as the Milky Way, but only 0.01 percent of the galaxy is made from ordinary visible matter; the rest is dark matter. The galaxy was discovered using the Dragonfly Telephoto Array in New Mexico, USA, which uses eight telephoto lenses to find objects in space that other telescopes can't find. Astronomers could see a huge galaxy that seemed to have hardly any stars until they realised that dark matter was holding the galaxy together.

88
Ra — 226
RADIUM
[Rn] 7s^2

84
Po — 209
POLONIUM
[Xe] 4f^{14}5d^{10}6s^{2}6p^4

MARIE AND PIERRE CURIE

Marie Curie and her husband Pierre worked on some of the most groundbreaking scientific research of their day, in the late 19th and early 20th centuries. They were the first people to use the term 'radioactivity' and their work changed the face of physics and chemistry. Marie was the first person to win the Nobel Prize twice (first in 1903 and again in 1911), and was the first woman to become a professor at the University of Paris.

Marie (originally Maria Skłodowska) was from Poland. She met French physicist Pierre Curie in Paris in 1894, where they bonded over their shared passion for physics and soon fell in love. Friends said at the time that Marie was 'Pierre's biggest discovery'. Pierre and Marie had a happy marriage, and they loved working together on their scientific dreams.

Marie studied how the rays coming from uranium, a chemical element, could conduct electricity and realised that the radiation energy was coming from the uranium atom itself, not from anything reacting with the uranium. Pierre and Marie looked at other minerals that contained uranium (called pitchblende and torbernite), and found that small quantities of these minerals were more radioactive than uranium. This meant that they contained powerful new elements that had not been discovered yet. Pierre and Marie discovered two new highly radioactive elements, one which they named 'polonium' after Marie's native Poland, and the other 'radium' after the Latin word for 'ray'.

It was incredibly hard to isolate pure radium and polonium. Marie and Pierre took pitchblende, which is a mineral created during silver mining, and processed tonnes of it to find very small amounts of radium. A tonne of pitchblende would only produce one tenth of a gram of radium. Different chemical processes were needed to separate the element, and it was a long and difficult task.

Because they were still discovering the principles of radioactivity, Marie and Pierre did not properly protect themselves from the dangerous elements that they were handling. They both experienced radiation sickness and radiation burns – when a radioactive element acts so strongly with a human that it burns the skin. All of their papers from the 1890s are so radioactive that they are too dangerous to touch and are kept in lead-lined boxes. Even Marie's cookbooks are too radioactive to handle. Pierre died in an accident in 1906 when he was hit by a horse-drawn cart when crossing the street in Paris. Marie died in 1934 from poisoning related to her exposure to the radioactive elements that had become her life's work.

As well as making huge scientific discoveries, Marie changed the idea of what a scientist looked like. Women were not well represented in science at the time, and she showed that a woman could make important discoveries and win the most prestigious prize in science, twice.

MEDICINE
PENICILLIN

Penicillin is an antibiotic, which is used to fight bacteria and infections. Penicillin is one of the most important discoveries of modern medicine and has saved millions of lives. It took a great many people working together to get penicillin to people who need it, all over the world.

In 1928 Scottish doctor Alexander Fleming discovered penicillin by accident. He returned home from holiday to check on experiments that he was conducting and saw that a green mould had contaminated some of the Petri dishes in his lab and had killed some of the bacteria he had grown. Alexander was able to isolate the mould and recreate the experiment showing him that this mould could kill a certain type of bacteria. Alexander's first name for his discovery was 'mould juice', which thankfully was later changed to penicillin, after the Latin name for the mould *Penicillium notatum*.

Though this was a medical breakthrough, at first Alexander found it very hard to convince other doctors of the importance of his discovery. It took many scientists to develop penicillin to the stage where it was able to get to the people who needed it and start saving lives. Alexander's discovery was groundbreaking, but hard to mass produce. More productive strains of Penicillium needed to be found, along with methods

for stabilisation and mass production.

In 1940 a research team of scientists at Oxford University, UK, led by Australian scientist Howard Florey, started to study the potential of penicillin. Howard and his colleague Ernst Chain discovered how to isolate the germ-killing agent in penicillin, but at first they could only produce this compound in very small quantities. The first successful medical use of penicillin was in 1942, when Harry Lambert (a friend of Alexander's brother) was cured of an infection of streptococcal meningitis, which would otherwise have been fatal. This

clinical trial was a huge success and proved that penicillin could cure bacterial infections. In 1945 Alexander, Howard and Ernst shared the Nobel Prize for their work on penicillin.

The next challenge was to mass produce penicillin in sufficient quantities so that it would be available for everyone that needed it. Howard and Alexander did not patent penicillin, thinking that would make it easier to treat people. In the US, Howard worked with scientists to find different

moulds that could produce more penicillin, and after a worldwide search, a mouldy cantaloupe melon from an Illinois market was found to have the best strain for mass production! By 1945 over 646 billion units of penicillin were being produced each year, and in 2015 nearly 35 billion doses of antibiotics were given out every day.

COVID VACCINE INVENTION

When the world was hit by a once-in-a-lifetime pandemic in 2020, scientists all around the world stepped up, working together to develop vaccines to protect against the deadly coronavirus disease (COVID-19). The main vaccines in wide use around the world are produced by Pfizer/BioNTech, Oxford/AstraZeneca, Moderna and Janssen. The Pfizer/BioNTech and Moderna vaccines use mRNA technology, where the vaccine delivers a small piece of code to your cells, which acts as an instruction manual for your immune system, telling it how to fight COVID-19.

The Pfizer/BioNTech vaccine was developed by husband-and-wife team, Dr Uğur Şahin and Dr Özlem Türeci, who have been studying mRNA for the last 25 years. Both born to Turkish parents, Dr Uğur and Dr Özlem grew up in Germany and met while at the same university. Together, they created a medical research company called BioNTech. When the coronavirus first started to spread, they decided to dedicate their entire company to creating an mRNA-based COVID vaccine, even though nothing like this had ever been done before.

With their entire company on the line, they approached the huge biopharmaceutical company Pfizer with an offer to

create a vaccine. Pfizer looked at the offer and said no.

At first, executives at Pfizer turned down Dr Uğur and Dr Özlem's offer to create a vaccine because they didn't think that coronavirus was going to be a widespread problem and would be easily controlled. Dr Uğur and Dr Özlem had studied reports on the virus and knew how quickly it could spread, and how serious the outbreak was going to be. Within weeks, executives at Pfizer changed their minds and work started on the vaccine.

Pfizer's calculations estimate that the research and development costs for the vaccine are close to $1 billion. The Pfizer/BioNTech vaccine is 90 percent effective, which is far higher than most jabs that are used for seasonal flu. The success also means that as the virus changes and mutates into new variants, the vaccine can also be updated to deal with them. There is also potential that treatments for diseases like cancer, tuberculosis (TB), HIV and malaria could also be created using the same system. However, Dr Uğur and

Dr Özlem are keen to point out that this is not easy, as all diseases are different and affect people in different ways.

Billions of shots of vaccines have been administered all over the world, which have saved millions of lives and allowed the world to start to return to normal. Thanks to the collaboration of many scientists around the world, medical science and the creation of a vaccine against COVID-19 advanced at lightspeed, and now we are much further ahead in our battle to beat the virus.

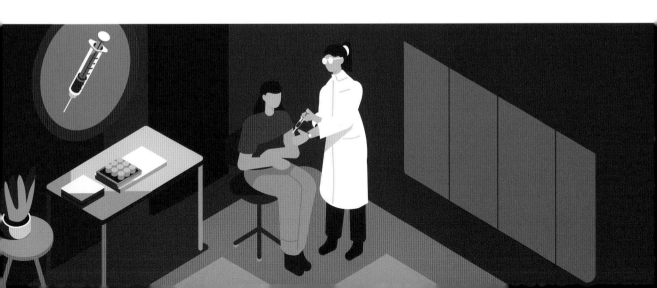

LOUIS AND MARIE PASTEUR

Louis and Marie Pasteur's greatest achievement was proving that germs spread diseases. At the time, there were a lot of theories about how diseases spread, including through smell, evil spirits, bad thoughts or even through the new technology of telephone wires. Louis and Marie showed that bacteria did not spontaneously appear and proved it only spreads and grows under the right conditions. More importantly, they showed that the spread of bacteria can be stopped.

Marie and Louis met in Strasbourg, France. Marie was the daughter of the university's rector and Louis was professor of chemistry. They were married in 1849 and had five children, but three children died of typhoid so only two survived to adulthood. The shock of these tragedies spurred Louis to search for a way to stop the spread of diseases, and to try to stop anything like this happening to another family. Marie worked with Louis on his most important scientific experiments and helped him expand his research. While there have been many husband-and-wife teams in science, no two are exactly the same. Marie was Louis' assistant and

liquids killed most of the bacteria, which would reduce the number of diseases they contained and make them safer to consume, while also lasting longer after they cooled down. Louis gave his name to this process – it is called pasteurisation and is still used on many items we eat and drink today, including milk, cheese, wine and juice.

The battle against diseases also led Louis to develop the first vaccines. Louis had the idea to cultivate a very weak form of a disease, then inject someone with that weak version so that they would be much better at fighting off the full version of the disease. The first vaccine was given to a nine-year-old boy called Joseph Meister, who had been bitten by a rabid dog and was in danger of getting rabies. The treatment was a success and Joseph did not develop rabies.

The work done by Louis and Marie is still incredibly relevant today, as their work forms the basis of many vaccines, and has helped to almost completely eradicate some diseases, such as polio. Today, the Pasteur Institute in Paris, France, carries on Louis and Marie's work through the study of biology, diseases, vaccines and micro-organisms.

co-worker; she took detailed scientific notes and made sure the necessary materials were available for experiments. She was known to be an important part of the scientific work by Louis' colleagues.

One of the most important processes that Louis discovered is one that we still use today. Louis knew that bacteria microbes were causing moulds to grow in liquids, like milk and wine. He found that heating the

INTERNATIONAL RED CROSS AND RED CRESCENT MOVEMENT

The Red Cross is an international organisation created to protect lives and bring medical care where it is needed most. It has about 14 million volunteers worldwide, all working together to try to prevent suffering and provide help to people in need.

The Red Cross was formed in 1863 after Swiss businessman Henry Dunant saw how horrific war was. He was shocked at how many people died needlessly on the battlefield and vowed to help. Henry proposed setting up neutral relief societies who would help wounded people during battles, regardless of who they were fighting for, or what they had done. He brought together a committee of representatives from different countries, and the idea started to spread all over the world.

Henry also wanted an international agreement that set out a number of rules about how countries treated doctors and the wounded on the battlefield. This agreement, first adopted in 1864, became known as the Geneva Convention and is still one of the most important pieces of law about how countries act during times of war. These laws were later updated to make sure that prisoners of war were treated in a civilised manner and not tortured.

There are 192 different Red Cross societies, one in nearly every country of the world, making up the International Federation of Red Cross and Red Crescent Societies. Each of these societies is different, but it is important that they are all treated equally. The fundamental principles of the Red Cross societies are that they are impartial and neutral and bring help to anyone who needs it. Their aim is to promote mutual understanding, friendship, cooperation and lasting peace.

The Red Cross does not just operate in war zones, it also offers disaster relief and emergency medical services. Red Cross societies have set up large scale vaccination projects, which are a vital tool in the fight against infectious diseases, including COVID-19. These types of mass immunisation programmes have meant that diseases like smallpox have been eradicated, and other diseases

like polio and measles have had transmission greatly reduced. Hundreds of millions of people died from smallpox in the 20th century but now the virus only

exists in two secure laboratories in Russia and the US.

The International Federation of Red Cross and Red Crescent Societies is an incredible example of what can happen when people from all over the world come together for a common good. The organisation has won the Nobel Peace Prize three times and continues to provide humanitarian aid all over the world.

1990

HUMAN GENOME PROJECT

Genome is the name for all our genetic information. It is the blueprint that contains the information about who we are and how we are made. Genes are made up of DNA (see page 16 for the discovery of DNA) and all our genes together are known as our genome. Your DNA is about 99.9 percent the same as any other human being, so the difference in genomes is very subtle. The Human Genome Project was a massive, international collaborative research programme which

allowed scientists to read and understand the complete genetic instruction manual for a human being for the first time. When the first sequence was shared in June 2000, the US President, Bill Clinton, called it 'the most important, most wondrous map ever produced by humankind.'

The Human Genome Project began in 1990 and was set up in the National Centre for Human Genome Research in the US. However, the actual work of

studying and sequencing DNA took place at universities and research centres all over the world, with researchers from the US, UK, France, Germany, Japan and China all sharing results. It took 13 years and nearly $3 billion to put the map of a human together.

Francis Collins, who was the director of the National Human Genome Research Institute, said that mapping the genome is like reading a book. He explained, 'It's a history book.

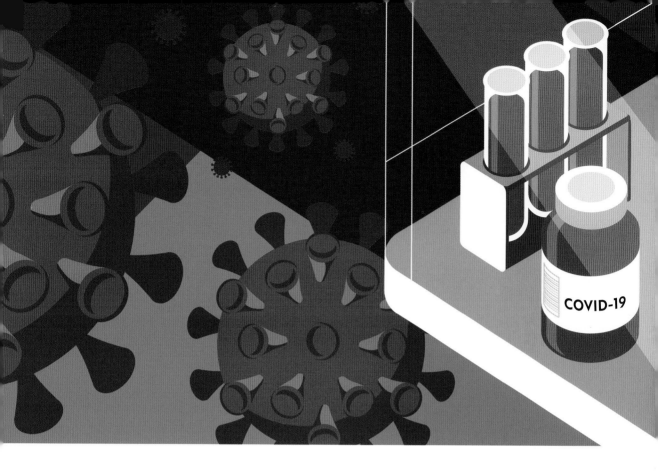

A narrative of the journey of our species through time. It's a shop manual, with an incredibly detailed blueprint for building every human cell. And it's a transformative textbook of medicine, with insights that will give health care providers immense new powers to treat, prevent and cure disease.'

The way that the information about the genome is shared is almost as important as the work itself. The Human Genome Project is not owned by anyone, and every part of the genome that was sequenced was made public as soon as it was found, with new information about the genome posted almost every day. When the project began, sharing data before the results were published wasn't the normal way for scientists to operate, and this project showed the benefits of scientific collaboration and information sharing.

The Human Genome Project has been incredibly important in the fight against COVID-19. Thanks to work completed as part of the project, it is relatively easy to map the sequence of a virus and to track it. This also means scientists can follow how a virus spreads and evolves, and see why it affects some people differently to others. Knowledge of the human genome has also meant huge advances in other areas, including the study of cancer, diabetes and migraines.

MOVABLE TYPE AND THE PRINTING REVOLUTION

Creating the printed word is one of the most important events in the history of mankind. Printing information means that it can be shared across continents and centuries, and books have remained relatively similar for hundreds of years.

Movable type was created by Chinese inventor Bi Sheng around 1040 AD. It is a system where letters and numbers can be moved around and then fixed in place, dipped in ink and then pressed on paper to leave a mark. These machines were first used to create books, and then to create money with different numbers on the notes so people could tell them apart.

The oldest surviving book created using movable type was printed in Korea in 1377. Before the invention of movable type, all books were made by copying pages out by hand, which took a very long time. As the books created by this new invention spread throughout the world, people came together to see how they could use printed paper to share information. In the Muslim world, movable type was developed further and was used to print many different types of books, including passages from the Qur'an.

In Germany in 1440 Johannes Gutenberg invented the printing press, which combined the idea of a screw press (which had been used to press things like wine) with movable type. Johannes partnered with Andreas Dritzen (a gem cutter) and Andreas Heilmann (the owner of a paper mill) to create the first printing press. Instead of being able to create 40 pages a day, a press could create 240 pages an hour, and much more cheaply. The first book printed by his printing press was the Gutenberg Bible.

Johannes's invention was the beginning of the printing revolution, and the printing press spread quickly across Europe and the rest of the world. Johannes didn't live to see the huge impact of his work; by 1500 printing presses were in over 270 cities around the world and over 20 million books had been printed. The presses then spread so rapidly that by 1600 between 150 and 200 million books had been printed!

The printing revolution introduced the era of mass communication, permanently changing society. It meant that people could spread information and ideas much more quickly and in ways that had never been seen before. One great example of this is that scientists were able to use printed journals to come together and form a community to share scientific ideas, which helped to start the scientific revolution in Europe in the late 1500s and early to mid 1600s.

This new printing revolution also meant that books were much more readily available, which led to a massive rise in literacy and education. In the past, ordinary workers had relied on priests and landowners to give them information, as most books were published in Latin and could only be read by the privileged elite. Now, people wanted to read in their own language and study ideas on their own. The printing press changed the world by getting more books in people's hands, allowing them to understand more about the world around them. The results of the printing revolution are still seen to this day – including the book that you hold in your hands right now!

THOMAS EDISON'S INVENTION FACTORY

Thomas Edison is considered one of the world's most prolific inventors and his name is on 1093 patents. Most of the inventions that were attributed to him came from his research laboratory, known as 'the invention factory'. This was the first industrial research laboratory, a place where teams of inventors could work together to spark wild and brilliant new ideas.

The invention factory was based in Menlo Park, New Jersey, USA and Thomas was given the nickname 'the Wizard of Menlo Park' by a newspaper reporter at the time. The invention factory grew, becoming so large it took up the same area as two city blocks. The first big invention to come from Menlo Park was the phonograph. This invention could record sounds and conversation, amazing the public at the time. Thomas was described as a 'genius' in a newspaper, but he relied on his team of inventors.

filament for the light bulb in 1881, which gave it a much longer life and made it more efficient. Lewis did not work in the invention factory, but he was the only Black member of 'Edison Pioneers', a group of men who had worked with Thomas and met up regularly once they had left.

Although Thomas didn't invent the light bulb, through Lewis's work he did manage to improve on the original electric versions, which were expensive and did not last long. Thomas set up an electric light factory in 1881 to profit on this new light bulb and started providing electric indoor lights to customers in New York. By 1882, he had installed over 10,000 electric lamps. He also lit Crystal Palace in London, UK as part of the 1882 International Electric Exhibition.

Thomas's legacy is vast, and much of it is thanks to the people that he brought together. Many people who worked for him later went on to do great things. They include Henry Ford, the founder of the Ford Motor Company, and Nikola Tesla, whose work on electricity forms the basis of the way that energy is sent to our homes today.

Thomas wanted to make sure that his inventors had everything they could ever need and demanded that the lab had a stock of almost every material available. Other inventions that came from the invention factory improved and updated existing ideas. Thomas patented a new and improved microphone for telephones. The telephone had only recently been invented by Alexander Graham Bell, and Thomas's carbon microphone made the sound clearer and easier to transmit.

Lewis Latimer was a talented inventor who began working for one of Thomas's rivals, later working for Thomas himself. Lewis created a new type of

THE WRIGHT BROTHERS

Orville and Wilbur Wright invented, built and flew the world's first powered aeroplane on 17 December 1903. Although human history is full of people who used gliders, hot air balloons and even kites to soar through the air, this was the first time that a powered machine had achieved flight and was the start of a century of air travel.

The Wright brothers had previously tried to fly on 14 December 1903. They had tossed a coin to see who would pilot their aeroplane (known as the Wright Flyer) and Wilbur had won. Unfortunately, he climbed too steeply on take-off, which meant he stalled and fell from the air, landing heavily and damaging the plane.

Once the plane had been repaired it was Orville's turn to fly on 17 December. Men from the local lifeboat station had been brought in to witness the event and help in case of emergency. One of these men, John T Daniels, saw the Wright brothers pause before the flight; remembering later, 'After a while they shook hands, and we couldn't help notice how they held on to each other's hand, sort o'like they hated to let go; like two folks parting who weren't sure they'd ever see each other again.'

The flight only lasted 12 seconds but history had been made. A human had flown. The brothers flew again three times that day, with Wilbur flying for 59 seconds and covering 260 m (852 ft) on the final flight of the day. This proved that their machine was capable of sustained, controlled flight. The importance of their achievement is not just that they flew, but that they had a system of aerodynamic control which allowed them to pilot the powered machine while in the air.

Orville and Wilbur then toured the world, demonstrating their rebuilt flyers to amazed crowds. While some were cynical at first, the brothers soon won them over with incredible feats of aeronautic display; flying high over crowds and even performing complex manoeuvres like figure of eight turns. Flying at the time was very dangerous and Orville was badly injured in a plane crash a few years later in 1908, spending several weeks in hospital. However, this did not deter Wilbur, who went on to perform for royalty all over Europe. For a while, Orville and Wilbur were two of the most famous people in the world and were followed everywhere by newspaper reporters and photographers.

Their invention changed the 20th century, transforming both commercial travel and military strategy. By showing that mechanical, controlled flight was possible, they found a way of bringing people together and making the world more connected.

APPLE INC.

Steve Jobs and Steve Wozniak met in California in the 1970s and bonded over a love of electronics and playing pranks on their friends. They founded Apple Computer Company in 1976 when Jobs was 21 and Wozniak was 26. Jobs wanted to change the world, while Wozniak cared about designing exciting new computers. They worked well as a team because Jobs was great at design, advertising and talking to the press, while Wozniak was more interested in creating computer systems. Wozniak didn't want to start a company at first, but Jobs talked him into taking a chance.

In 1976 the Apple Computer Company launched their first computer which was called the Apple I. The Apple I was quite basic by today's standards – it was a circuit board that didn't even come with a keyboard, monitor or case. To raise money for parts to create these computers, Jobs sold his Volkswagen van and Wozniak sold his expensive HP scientific calculator. The first computers were put together in Jobs' parents' house and sometimes in their garage. The Apple I sold well enough for Jobs and Wozniak to create the Apple II, which came with a case, a keyboard and two games controllers. The Apple II computer was launched in 1977 under the newly named Apple Computer, Inc. and was the first personal computer to display colour graphics. It became one

of the first successful mass-produced home computers and within a few years, Jobs and Wozniak were millionaires.

But Jobs did not stop there. He realised that computers would need computer graphics and not just text, so he and his team developed the Apple Macintosh, a personal computer which had icons for users to click on with a mouse, rather than having to type text commands on a keyboard. The Apple team created the basics of how we interact with computers today.

Apple Computer, Inc. grew over the next few years, with a talented team of programmers, software engineers and technicians working together to make it one of the biggest companies in the world. Jobs and Wozniak had sold shares in Apple to get money to grow the company and create the team that they needed. Apple had grown so large that in 1985 the board of directors was able to remove Jobs from the company that he had co-founded. Wozniak also left Apple, partially because he felt he was no longer needed, and partially because he missed the fun of the early days. Jobs created a new company called NeXT that same year. The first product was released in 1988 and the company was bought by Apple in 1997, bringing Jobs back in charge of his old team again.

Jobs and his team steered the company while they released ground-breaking products that are now household names, from the iPod and MacBook to the iPhone and iPad. They understood the importance of clear, uncomplicated design and changed how we interact with technology.

Today, Apple Inc. is worth over $2 billion and in 2021 was the largest company in the world. Jobs died from pancreatic cancer in 2011, leaving a legacy which changed the first decade of the 21st century. Wozniak is still employed by Apple Inc. and is a shareholder in the company.

THE INTERNAL COMBUSTION ENGINE

TECHNOLOGY

The history of the invention of the internal combustion engine is spread over many years, with a succession of inventors taking the concept and developing it further. The individual parts that would eventually make up the engine took centuries to come together. Sometimes human ingenuity is demonstrated when inventors improve on an idea, working together over time by building on each other's work.

Internal combustion engines have formed the basis for most powered vehicles for over a century. From cars to jet planes, the internal combustion engine works by igniting a fuel (often petrol) and air mixture, which pushes a moving piston on a fixed crank, creating energy to power the vehicle. The first pistons to use ignition to fire were developed in Southeast Asia before 350 BCE, while the crank operating system has been around in China for almost as long. The gas turbine was patented by English inventor John Barber in 1791, but it wasn't until 1807 that engines were able to propel vehicles. Brothers Nicéphore and Claude Niépce used an engine to power a boat, while in that same year Swiss engineer François Isaac de Rivaz used a spark powered engine to drive a carriage, calling it 'the world's first internal combustion engine powered automobile'.

The most famous form of internal combustion engine is the diesel engine, created by Rudolf Diesel in 1892. He made a machine that wasted as little energy as possible thanks to the compression levels inside the engine. The diesel engine gives its name to diesel fuel, which is refined from crude oil, but the first engine was actually run on peanut oil! The high levels of fuel efficiency make diesel engines a good choice for heavy equipment like trucks, lorries or trains. These engines weren't only used to power vehicles, they could also be used to automate hard, back-breaking manual labour jobs. The first commercial diesel engine was built by a brewing company in America in 1898, and within a few years thousands of diesel engines were in service.

The internal combustion engine is used in many powered land and sea vehicles, as well as most cars. It changed the 20th century because it made long distance travel a much more practical possibility. Journeys that took days by horse could now be completed in hours by car. The internal combustion engine literally brought people together like no invention had done before, allowing personal transport and freedom on a previously unseen scale.

TECHNOLOGY
TETRIS

Tetris is one of the most popular games ever created. It has sold over 200 million copies and holds the Guinness World Records title for most ported video game, meaning that it has appeared on the highest number of different platforms. It's a deceptively simple game where the player has to stack falling tiles of different shapes to complete a row, which then disappears. Tetris isn't just fun to play, research suggests that it could even be good for your brain, resulting in a thicker cortex (processing centre) and increased brain activity.

The first version of Tetris was created in 1984 by Russian

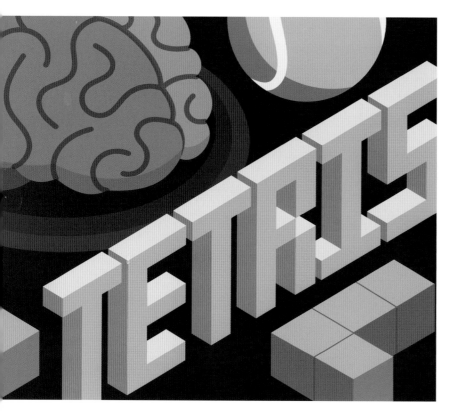

computer programmer Alexey Pajitnov, who got the name Tetris from combining the words 'tetra' (meaning four) and 'tennis' (his favourite sport). He programmed the game on a very early computer called the Elektronika 60, which was so basic it did not even have colour graphics. Alexey was working in the Soviet Academy of Sciences at the time, and his colleagues loved the new game he had created. News of this addictive game spread through Moscow and Alexey's friend Vladimir Pokhilko had to ban the game from the Moscow Medical Institute because people were stopping work to play it. In Russia there was no market for computer games, so Alexey would give away copies of the game on floppy disks.

Alexey had something special but he needed the help of others to make it a hit. He asked a 16-year-old programmer called Vadim Gerasimov to help him adapt the game for the IBM PC which was one of the most widely used computers at the time. Vadim added coloured

pieces and a scoreboard to the game. Alexey's friend, Vladimir, helped him develop the game further and later worked with Alexey on marketing it around the world.

Tetris was a massive hit but it took a while for Alexey to make any money from his creation. Tetris was one of the first games for Nintendo's handheld console, the Game Boy, and sold millions of copies. However, the licensing deal that Alexey had signed meant he didn't get any of the money at first. Still, Alexey was proud of his game, saying that he wanted to use computers to make people happy.

In 1996, Alexey got control of Tetris again and now receives money from every copy of the

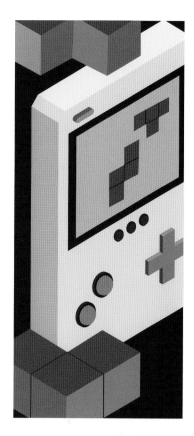

game that is sold. Dutch video game designer Henk Rogers helped Alexey regain control of the rights and now works with him as Managing Director of The Tetris Company. Alexey also has control of any new versions of the game and he works with his partners at The Tetris Company to make sure that all versions of Tetris are made to the highest quality.

THE WORLD WIDE WEB

The internet is a huge network of computers, but this would be useless without the World Wide Web. The World Wide Web is a collection of web pages which are stored on the internet and accessed using a web browser. The brilliance is that it will only work if computers all over the world understand each other.

English scientist Sir Tim Berners-Lee invented the basis for the World Wide Web in 1989 and it has been updated and improved on by many other programmers since. Sir Tim wanted to find a way for scientists to easily share data from their experiments. He was working at the CERN research institute at the time and was frustrated that information couldn't be shared between different computers.

Sir Tim was not working on his own. One of the most important parts of the World Wide Web was the creation of hypertext – words that bring you to another web page or file when clicked on. He worked with Belgian computer scientist Robert Cailliau to formalise how hypertext would work and Robert ensured that hypertext would function across different computers. Computers use Hypertext Transfer Protocol (HTTP) to communicate with each other and this forms the basis of the World Wide Web. Sir Tim also suggested using HyperText Markup Language (HTML) as the universal language for writing websites and Uniform Resource Locators (URLs), which are more commonly known as web addresses, as a way of finding websites.

Websites are held on web servers and the first server was created by Sir Tim in 1990. It soon demonstrated the importance of teamwork and collaboration. Sir Tim asked developers to help him expand the internet further and in 1991 the first server outside of Europe was created by Paul Kunz and Louise Addis at Stanford University in California. Soon, new servers had been created by teams all over the world. By the end of 1994, the internet had gone from one to 10,000 servers, with 10 million users.

In 1993 CERN made the source code available on a royalty free basis. The fundamental principle of the World Wide Web is that it is free for everyone to use and is not owned by anybody. The Web is so important because it

```
1    <!doctype html>
2    <html lang="en">
3        <head>
4            <title>worl
5        </head>
6        <body>
7            <h1>Tim Be
8            <p> Invento
9            <p>
10           <p> Share k
11           <p>
12           <p> Free fo
13           <p>
14           <p> Conne
```

Tim Berners-Lee @timberners_lee
This is for everyone #london2012 #oneweb

↩ Reply ⇄ Retweet ★ Favorite

allows computers and users to interact in one single, universal space. This provides the basis for nearly unlimited collaboration and teamwork on the internet.

Sir Tim was part of the Opening Ceremony for the London 2012 Olympic Games, which showcased great British inventions. As part of the ceremony, Sir Tim tweeted 'This is for everyone', referring to the guiding philosophy of the World Wide Web.

Still, Sir Tim sees room for the Web to grow, saying, 'The Web as I envisaged it, we have not seen it yet. The future is still so much bigger than the past.'

THE BLACK MAMBA ANTI-POACHING UNIT

The Black Mamba Anti-Poaching Unit is a ranger unit which mainly operates in the Balule Nature Reserve in South Africa. Their mission is to protect wildlife including elephants, lions and rhinos from poachers, who illegally hunt and kill the animals for money. The Black Mamba APU is a nearly all-female unit and they have become heroes in their communities. They wear a distinctive uniform and each member spends 21 days a month on patrol.

The Mambas monitor and patrol the nature reserve, looking for signs of poaching. There are lots of different ways that poachers operate, so the Mambas have to work closely as a team. Duties include checking rhino watering holes for poison, looking for poacher camps and sweeping the reserve for snares, which are wire or cable traps designed to catch animals. A large part of their work is deterrence as their presence can help to keep poachers away. Since the unit started in 2013, they have shut down five poacher camps and reduced poaching in the nature reserve by 75 percent.

When the Black Mamba APU was first formed, many people didn't believe that a group of women could do a traditionally male job, but the team has been happy to prove them wrong. The unit was formed by Craig Spencer, the head warden of the nature reserve. The first members were scientists and

managers, but now many of the new recruits join after high school. Different companies sponsor the Mambas and some of the unit's funding comes from an environmental protection fund. The group grew from six to 26 members in just a few years. They do difficult work as they face dangers not only from poachers but also from deadly wildlife. The unit must train hard because they never know when they are going to come face-to-face with a lion or rhino.

Poaching is a serious problem in South Africa. Rhinos especially are sought after for their horns, which is pushing the animal closer and closer to extinction. Founding member NoCry Mzimba said that her reasons for joining the Black Mamba APU were simple, 'We want our children to be able to see and experience rhinos in the wild.'

The Mambas' work has been celebrated all over the world. The unit was given the Champions of the Earth Award in 2015 by the United Nations Environmental Program (UNEP), and in 2020 won the Earth Care Award from the Sierra Club, the oldest conservation organisation in the US.

The Mambas also run an education programme which teaches local children about wildlife and conservation. They hope to make poaching a thing of the past through education, inspiration and food security.

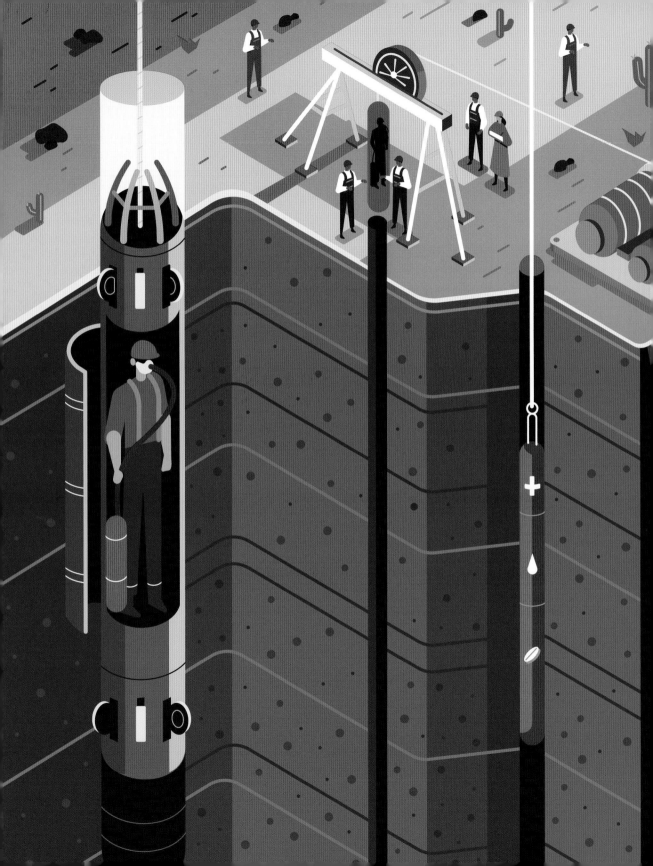

THE 2010 COPIAPÓ MINING ACCIDENT

On 5 August 2010 there was a catastrophic cave-in at the San José copper-gold mine near Copiapó in northern Chile. The collapse trapped 33 men underground, nearly 5 km (3 miles) from the mine's entrance and 700 m (2,300 ft) underground. The story of how these men were saved is about teamwork, cooperation and unity in the face of great danger.

At first, no-one knew what had happened to the miners after the cave-in, so rescue teams drilled holes into the mine to see if they could reach any survivors. Seventeen days after the accident when one of the drill bits was pulled back, it had a note attached to it, saying, 'We are well in the shelter, the 33.'

The 33 miners survived because they came together and worked as a disciplined and organised team. There were people of different ages, the youngest was Jimmy Sanchez, who was only 19 at the time, and the oldest was 59-year-old Mario Gomez, so they all took different roles. They divided themselves into three eight-hour shifts, with different teams taking responsibility for sanitation, preventing further rockfalls and environmental safety.

The miners had limited supplies and had been living on two mouthfuls of tuna and a sip of milk a day, with a few bites of cracker every other day. Each miner lost about 9 kg (20 lb) and became dangerously dehydrated. Once the miners were located, rescue teams could start to send down food, but they had to be careful that the miners did not put on too much weight, as they were about to be pulled out from under the earth.

Every part of the Chilean government began working on rescuing the trapped miners and they also called in NASA's Engineering and Safety Centre to help. The NASA team built two special capsules to lower into the mine, called Fenix 1 and Fenix 2. The capsules were long and thin, 4-m (13-ft) tall but only 53 cm (21 in) in diameter, because they had to navigate through very tight spaces. The capsule was fitted with audio and video links, an emergency oxygen supply and heart rate monitors. The aim was to bring the miners to the surface as quickly and safely as possible. The capsules even had trapdoors at the bottom in case the capsule got stuck and the miners needed to escape. Three different drilling rig teams drilled into the mine to make a hole big enough to rescue the miners, but they had to be very careful not to cause another cave-in.

On 13 October 2010, with the whole world watching, a rescue was attempted. The Fenix 2 capsule was lowered into the hole, a miner was strapped in, then it was pulled to the surface. Each trip took between 10 and 15 minutes. One by one, the miners were pulled to the surface after 69 days underground. 5.3 million people worldwide watched as the last man, crew foreman Luis Urzúa, was pulled up, completing the rescue. Amazingly, all 33 miners were in good health when they were pulled out as they had worked together to stay alive in the most difficult conditions.

WORLD WILDLIFE FUND FOR NATURE

The World Wildlife Fund for Nature (also known as the WWF) is the world's largest conservation organisation. Founded in 1961, it has invested over $1 billion in conservation projects around the world. It has a mission statement to stop the degradation of the planet, to conserve biological diversity, to promote the use of renewable natural resources and to promote the reduction of pollution and wasteful consumption.

The majority of the WWF's funding comes from donations, but some comes from government sources and corporations. There are lots of other ways the WWF has raised money, including several albums, books, magazines and even an environmental musical narrated by Sir David Attenborough. There are WWF offices all around the

world, but the organisation is based in Switzerland. The WWF works on global issues, collaborating with local groups and leaders on projects that promote conservation and sustainability as well as working with governments to create laws that protect biodiversity and natural resources.

The symbol of the WWF is an image of Chi Chi, a giant panda who came from Sichuan in China to live in London Zoo. The giant panda works as a symbol because it is an endangered species which benefits from the WWF's conservation efforts. As the economy in China grows on a global scale, the WWF is committed to working with the Chinese government and businesses on sustainable environmental and conservation targets.

The WWF was the first international conservation organisation invited to work in China. It has helped the Chinese government establish a giant panda conservation network with 62 giant panda nature reserves, which together cover over 1.34 million hectares – almost double the size of Shanghai.

The huge scale of the WWF means that it can employ the latest scientific research. WWF scientists research the impact of climate change around the world, trying to find ways to protect vulnerable people and species. Conservation projects can become real-world 'experiments' that allow scientists to look at how well different systems or interventions work, then fine-tune them to ensure the best impact. The WWF has worked for 60 years to protect communities, wildlife and habitats, but it can only do that when people work together. The World Wildlife Fund for Nature is a great example of people collaborating to find solutions to one of the biggest challenges facing the modern world.

CAMPOBELLO WHALE RESCUE TEAM

The Campobello Whale Rescue Team is dedicated to the protection and stewardship of whales in Canadian waters. The CWRT is part of the Canadian Whale Institute and is a highly skilled team made up of fishermen, biologists and scientists who study whales, whale behaviour and fishing.

Rescuing whales means working as a team, both in the water and on dry land. Members of Campobello Whale Rescue Team study the latest tactics for disentangling whales from fishing gear. The plan is not to indiscriminately cut the ropes or other traps that the whales are caught in, but instead to understand the nature of the problem then work as a team to come up with a plan. The team has a wide range of tools at its disposal, including grappling hooks, poles, fixed or flying knives, sea anchors and more. It is very dangerous for a whale to be entangled in fishing gear, as it can damage their health, prevent them from feeding and even kill them.

The CWRT was formed in 2002 by a group of volunteer fishermen who were concerned about the plight of Canadian whales and it has grown to

become a highly skilled team. Becoming a whale disentangler takes a lot of hard work, study and practice. Trainees go from being an Apprentice to Assistant to Small Whale Team Leader and finally to Expert Whale Disentangler. Only an expert may lead a team to disentangle a large whale. The CWRT also works with the US Government's Atlantic Large Whale Disentanglement Network.

The whale rescue team focuses on research as well as rescue and the team of scientists work together on the latest conservation projects. Their studies include maritime outreach initiatives, whale habitat management strategies and the study of ancient marine mammal DNA. The Campobello Whale Rescue Team also looks at the risks for North Atlantic whales from ocean-going vessels and fishing gear.

Education and outreach are an important part of the CWRT's work and they do not consider their work complete until the results of their research are shared with the general public, mariners and policy makers. The CWRT holds summer camps, gives presentations to local businesses and runs an information centre. One of the most important parts of the CWRT's brief is to work with the community so the team makes sure to have regular 'dockside chats' with fishermen, community members and other researchers. Working with the community is the best way for the Campobello Whale Rescue Team to accomplish its mission.

JANE GOODALL INSTITUTE

54

The Jane Goodall Institute was established in 1977 by English primatologist and anthropologist Jane Goodall. Jane has worked for over 60 years studying primates and their habitats, and her discovery in 1960 that chimpanzees make and use tools completely changed the way that we think about man's relationship to apes. However, the Jane Goodall Institute is about more than just Jane herself; it promotes a global message of conservation, protection and teamwork. The Institute now employs over 300 people, including field scientists, conservationists and trainers who work together with the same mission of protection. It has a huge global presence, with headquarters in Virginia in the US, and offices in more than 25 countries.

The Jane Goodall Institute takes a community-centred

approach to conservation, which means international and local collaboration. It works with local people who know their communities best as a way of advancing conservation where it is needed most. The Institute doesn't just work on conservation, it also promotes community-centred health projects, such as improvements to water supplies, and community programmes to keep girls in school. The Jane Goodall Institute's Girls Scholarship Project has assisted hundreds of girls with their education alongside conservation and development programmes in the community.

One of the most successful programmes run by the Institute is the Roots & Shoots Across Africa programme. Roots & Shoots was launched in Tanzania in 1991 by a group of 12 high school students who wanted to improve conservation efforts in their communities. With the help of the Jane Goodall Institute, they were able to grow the programme and now have more than 3,100 groups in African countries. Roots & Shoots groups run events and activities with a focus both on conservation and training, looking to empower the next generation of activists. The mission of Roots & Shoots is to empower young people to lead the charge in creating innovative solutions to the major issues in their communities.

The plight of chimpanzees and other primates is very important to the Jane Goodall Institute. The Institute runs sanctuaries to help primates and works with local efforts to reduce poaching and illegal trafficking. The Institute promotes public education about endangered primates through radio broadcasts, billboards, fact sheets and stickers.

The Jane Goodall Institute has the largest scientific knowledge base on chimpanzees and is consulted by primatologists all over the world. It is constantly expanding its research. Chimpanzees are mankind's closest living relatives and this work is invaluable in understanding their lives and behaviour. By building this understanding, the Institute strengthens the bond between primate and man.

THE MAGNA CARTA

The Magna Carta (which literally means 'the Great Charter' in Latin) is perhaps the most important item in English legal history and is one of the most famous documents in the world. Many of the legal freedoms we take for granted today stem from the Magna Carta. It is a brilliant example of people working together and creating something for the common good. A group of people united to challenge the King, achieving something that wouldn't have been possible as individuals.

In the year 1215, King John ruled England and he was not a popular king. He was a cruel man who did not think twice about imprisoning and killing his enemies without a trial – he even imprisoned his own wife! King John wanted to fight wars in France but wars are expensive as money is required for soldiers, weapons, food and armour. King John raised this money by imposing heavy taxes on his barons, who were the wealthy landowners at the time. If they didn't pay, he would imprison them, punish them or seize their property, all without a trial.

After returning from a particularly bloody battle in France, King John was confronted by 40 barons at Runnymede in England. They rebelled against King John, threatening civil war unless he met their demands. The group

had strength because of their numbers, so King John was forced to negotiate with them.

The result of these negotiations was written down, resulting in the document we know as the Magna Carta. The most important part of the Magna Carta is still part of the law in England today. It gave all men the right to justice and a fair trial, 'No man shall be arrested or imprisoned except by the judgement of their equals and by the law of the land.'

The Magna Carta has been hugely influential all over the world. During the American Revolution, the Magna Carta inspired the American colonists to fight for their freedom from the British. When the US Constitution was later written, the Magna Carta was the basis for many key rights, including the idea that no-one should be 'deprived of life, liberty, or property, without due process of law.' In 1941 in his inaugural address, President Roosevelt told the country, 'The democratic aspiration is no mere recent phase in human history... It was written in Magna Carta.'

The origins of the Magna Carta came from a group of barons banding together to stop what they saw as injustice, but has become an international symbol of liberty and a cornerstone of human rights.

1215

WOMEN'S SUFFRAGE

At the start of the 20th century, women did not have the right to vote in many countries, including the United Kingdom and the United States. Realising that the world would not change unless forced, women came together to demand women's suffrage – the right to vote.

Sarah Parker Redmond, a Black physician, moved to the UK from the US around 1856 and became an early campaigner for abolition and suffrage. The Women's Social and Political Union, led by Emmeline Pankhurst, was formed in 1903. The word 'suffragette' was initially used as an insult, but it soon became a badge of honour. The Suffragettes engaged in direct action and civil disobedience, with the motto 'deeds, not words'. Princess Sophia Duleep Singh was the daughter of the last Maharaja of the Sikh empire in Punjab, God-daughter to Queen Victoria and a close friend of Emmeline Pankhurst. Actively involved in the WSPU, Princess Sophia refused to pay taxes as a form of protest. The WSPU organised marches and printed leaflets, newspapers and posters, but they also advocated direct, and sometimes violent, protest. They tried to storm parliament, clashed with the police, chained themselves to railings, disrupted events and even carried out bombing and arson campaigns. Famously, activist Emily Davison tried to disrupt the 1913 Epsom Derby and was killed when she ran in front of the King's horse.

The campaign for women's suffrage in the United States was initially split between two organisations, the National Woman Suffrage Association and the American Woman Suffrage Association. However, the groups joined together in 1890 to form the National American Woman Suffrage Association, led by Susan B Anthony (who had been arrested for voting in 1872) and Elizabeth Cady Stanton. The organisations campaigned for women's voting rights both at a state and national level. The National Association of Colored Women was formed in 1896 and led by Mary Church Terrell. It fought against issues of civil rights and injustice, including suffrage. The NACW adopted the motto 'Lifting as we climb'. Ida B. Wells was a journalist and founding member of the National Association for the Advancement of Colored People. She fought for both race and gender equality at a time where many suffrage movements excluded women of colour, focusing only on the advancement of white women.

The outbreak of World War I in 1914 meant that suffrage paused on both sides of the Atlantic. The war caused many changes to society and countries including Germany, Austria, Poland and Lithuania adopted women's suffrage in 1918. In the UK, a law was passed in 1918 which allowed women over 30 who owned property to vote. It wasn't until 1928 that all women over 21 could vote, finally achieving the same voting rights as men.

Some states in the US had previously given women the right to vote, but in 1920 Congress passed the 19th Amendment to the Constitution, saying, 'The right of citizens of the United States to vote shall not be denied or abridged by the United States or by any State on account of sex.' However, in practice, many women were excluded on the basis of gender and race. Native American, Asian American, Latinx and African American suffragists continued the fight and true equal voting rights were not achieved until the 1960s.

THE MONTGOMERY BUS BOYCOTT

On 1 December 1955, seamstress Rosa Parks set off a chain of events that would play a key role in the ongoing Civil Rights Movement in the US. In Montgomery, Alabama in 1955, the law required Black people to give up their seats to white people in certain sections of public buses. As part of a planned protest against the unjust law, Rosa Parks refused to give up her seat to a white man and was arrested.

Nine months previously a 15-year-old named Claudette Colvin had also been arrested for refusing to give up her seat to a white person. However, being young, and subsequently becoming pregnant, some civil rights leaders felt that Claudette was not a good figurehead for the movement. Despite this, Claudette was involved in the federal civil action lawsuit that challenged Alabama's bus

segregation laws and would ultimately rule them unlawful.

At the time of her arrest, Rosa Parks was a long-time activist and member of the National Association for the Advancement of Colored People (NAACP). She worked with E. D. Nixon, the president of the Montgomery NAACP, to appeal her conviction and challenge segregation in Alabama. He brought together local ministers and political activist Dr. Martin Luther King, Jr. to organise a bus boycott in protest. The boycott called for Black people to not travel on public transport until they stopped the segregation of passengers. This was a risky tactic as it meant that many Black workers and students would have no form of transport and would have to walk for hours in hot and dangerous conditions. During the boycott, the community came together to work for a common cause – carpools were organised and taxis offered cheap fares.

The Montgomery Bus Boycott ended after 382 days when the Supreme Court ruled that Alabama's racial segregation laws for buses were unconstitutional and ordered them to stop. The Montgomery Bus Boycott soon became about more than

just desegregation of buses. It became the focus of the Civil Rights Movement and helped bring attention to Dr. Martin Luther King, Jr. who would go on to become a national figurehead and a shaping figure of the 20th century.

The boycott sparked a movement that was seen all over the world, inspiring other countries to act. In 1963 activists in the UK organised the Bristol Bus Boycott, campaigning against a Bristol bus company which would not employ Black or Asian bus crews. The boycott lasted for four months and resulted in the policy being overturned. The movement was influential in working towards reforming race relations in the UK.

BLACK LIVES MATTER: INTERNATIONAL MOVEMENT

Black Lives Matter is a movement and phrase used to draw attention to the racism and discrimination experienced by Black people, especially in their encounters with the state. The Black Lives Matter movement was started in the US by three Black women, Patrisse Cullors, Alicia Garza and Ayọ Tometi, but has been taken up around the world.

The movement was sparked after a 17-year-old boy called Trayvon Martin was killed by a man named George Zimmerman in Florida in 2012. After George Zimmerman was not charged with Trayvon's death, people came together to protest and call for justice. Protesters took to the streets in 2014 when two Black men, Michael Brown

and Eric Garner, were killed by police officers, and again in 2015 after the death of Sandra Bland while in police custody. Protesters called for an end to police violence, highlighting statistics that Black people are three times more likely to be shot by the police in the US, and are not treated equally in the criminal justice system.

In 2016 NFL star Colin Kaepernick began kneeling during the American national anthem as a

"I CAN'T BREATHE"

way of highlighting racial injustice and oppression. He faced backlash for the gesture and was not picked by any major NFL team the following season. Athletes and sports people have since followed Colin's lead by kneeling at the start of sporting events as a way of showing their opposition to racism. This is called 'taking a knee' and has been adopted by Premier League football teams in the UK.

In March 2020 26-year-old Breonna Taylor was shot and killed by police when they forced their way into her home during the night. Later that

year, a man named George Floyd was killed after a police officer knelt on his neck, suffocating him. The death was filmed by passers-by and seen all over the world. George's last words, 'I can't breathe' became a powerful mantra for the movement. These events sparked protests around the world, with hundreds of thousands of people marching against racism. In the UK, statues of slave-owners, including one of Edward Colston in Bristol, were pulled down in protest of commemorating historical figures involved in the slave trade.

Fighting racism, discrimination and inequality is difficult but everyone must speak out against injustice, even if it's difficult or comes from positions of power. Change can be achieved when people work together.

BLACK LIVES MATTER

#BLM

POLITICS AND ACTIVISM

CLIMATE CHANGE ACTIVISM

The dangers of climate change are beyond debate. The temperature of the Earth is rising and globally we must reduce the amount of carbon released into the atmosphere. Climate change activism takes the form of direct protest, education and political activism. There are many different activist groups who have been working to encourage meaningful action on climate change.

The School Strike for Climate is an international youth movement which demands that political leaders take action to prevent climate change. Also known as Fridays For Future, school students skip classes on Fridays to raise awareness for the cause. The School Strike movement came to international attention in August 2018 when 15-year-old Swedish pupil Greta Thunberg held a protest outside the Swedish parliament. The movement grew and in 2019 millions of people took part in the largest climate strikes in history. Thousands of scientists have signed a letter supporting the school strikes, writing 'concerns of young protesters are justified [...] and supported by the best available science.'

Tackling climate change means making political changes and the Sunrise Movement is an American political action organisation committed to

making these changes. The Sunrise Movement works to elect politicians who will back renewable and cleaner energy sources. The movement has organised sit-ins in various politicians' offices, where activists have demanded that politicians stop taking money from companies that create fossil fuels. The Sunrise Movement is fighting for a Green New Deal, a piece of legislation designed to tackle the climate crisis, create millions of clean jobs and help the communities most affected by the climate crisis.

Coming together as part of a global movement for climate action also means thinking about our own personal choices. Things like the food we eat, how we travel and the products we buy all affect the environment. Big changes, like living without a car, reducing the amount of plane journeys we take, buying more sustainable products and moving to a plant-based diet can have a big impact. However, these personal changes must be accompanied by action from big businesses and governments.

Although the reality of climate change can make it seem like an enormous and scary topic with no solution in sight, the huge levels of activism and demand for action are incredible. Politicians and corporations are starting to listen to a new generation of young climate change activists. As the Global Climate Strike team puts it, 'There is hope in the leadership of our young people, in our collective power and in our unwavering faith in justice.'

THE UNITED NATIONS

In 1945 the world had been ravaged by World War II and, while the remaining big powers didn't agree on much, they could all agree that they wanted to prevent any more global wars. The League of Nations, which had been founded after World War I to prevent wars, had obviously been ineffective and a larger, more collaborative organisation was needed. The United States, United Kingdom, Soviet Union and Republic of China worked to create the structure for an organisation for world peace. In April 1945 they invited other nations to the UN Conference on International Organization in San Francisco, USA, where the Charter of the United Nations was created over two months.

The United Nations started with 51 member states in 1945 and has grown to 193 member states today. The UN's mission is to be the one place on Earth where representatives from all the world's nations can gather to discuss common problems and try to find shared solutions. Any country can join the UN as long as they follow the rules of the UN charter and are voted in by the other countries. The headquarters for the United Nations are in New York City, and it has buildings in Geneva, Vienna and Nairobi. All these buildings are designated as international territory, meaning they do not belong to the country they are found in.

The importance of the UN comes not just from what it can do, but what it represents. The UN is not a government and has no right to make laws – its most important power comes from diplomacy, cooperation and negotiation. UN committees work together on agreements which, when combined, form a body of international law. Every country that is a member of the UN is able to vote in the General Assembly meeting, so everyone gets a say in the decisions that are made.

The UN's key objectives are to maintain international peace and to uphold international law. The UN is also committed to protecting human rights, delivering humanitarian aid, disaster relief, counterterrorism and trying to reduce the amount of nuclear weapons in the world. The UN peacekeeping force can send troops where they are needed in the world to keep the peace, operating within a strict set of mandates set by the UN Security Council and General Assembly.

While not everyone agrees with every UN decision, the UN (and its related agencies and staff) have been awarded the Nobel Peace Prize twelve times, with the Nobel prize committee saying, 'The only negotiable route to global peace and cooperation goes by way of the United Nations.'

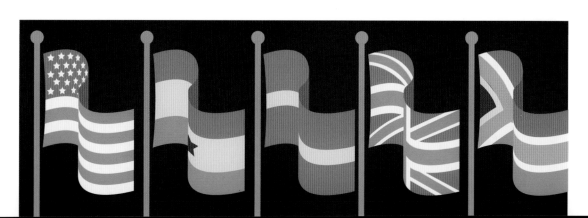

The Olympic Games started in ancient Greece over 3,000 years ago and, after a break of a few hundred years, were revived in the 19th century. We don't know when exactly the first Olympic Games were held, but there are records dating back to 776 BC. The Greek legend is that they were founded by Heracles (called Hercules by the Romans) as a way of honouring the god Zeus.

Unlike the modern Games, the ancient Olympic Games did not move around, but were held in the city of Olympia, which gave the Games their name. Like the modern Games, the ancient Olympic Games were held every four years. They were very important in the ancient world and sacrifices would be made to the Greek god Zeus. During the Games, there would be an Olympic truce between warring nations so that athletes could travel safely to and from Olympia. Even so, the Games were a political event and would be used in negotiations by nations and nation states. At their most popular, over 40,000 people attended the Games each day, bringing people together through their love of sport.

There were fewer events in the ancient Olympic Games than there are today. They included running events, boxing, wrestling, pankration (a no-holds-barred martial arts competition, a bit like MMA), horse and chariot racing and a pentathlon. The Greek pentathlon consisted of javelin, discus, wrestling, running and jumping. Athletes competed naked, which would certainly make events harder to televise if it was still the case today!

Over the years the ancient Games slowly fell into disrepute. In 67 AD, Roman emperor Nero took part in a chariot race and, even

THE OLYMPIC GAMES

though he fell off his chariot, he declared himself the winner. The Olympic Games continued for centuries, until they were banned by the Roman emperor Theodosius, who said they were a 'pagan' festival.

Over 1,500 years later, a French Baron called Pierre de Coubertin proposed bringing back the Games. He brought together an International Olympic Committee and in 1896 the first modern Olympic Games were held in Greece. The popularity of the Games grew – the very first Winter Olympics for snow and ice sports was held in 1924 and the Paralympic Games for athletes with disabilities was introduced in 1960. When first brought back, Pierre saw the possibility for the games to bring people together, saying, 'Olympism is a

destroyer of dividing walls. It calls for air and light for all.'

The official symbol of the modern Olympic Games is five interlocking, coloured rings, symbolising the continents of Africa, Asia, Australia, Europe and North and South America. Over 200 teams take part in the Olympic Games, with more than 11,200 athletes competing. Over three billion people watch the Games, which is

slightly less than half the world's population! While modern sporting events like skateboarding and table tennis would probably seem strange to ancient Olympians, the sense of sporting achievement, teamwork and community would not.

UEFA (UNION OF EUROPEAN FOOTBALL ASSOCIATIONS)

One of the most important footballing associations in the world, UEFA (Union of European Football Associations) runs the biggest tournaments and competitions in Europe. It runs the UEFA European Championship tournament, as well as several football leagues including the UEFA Nations League and the UEFA Champions League. Created in 1954, the founders of UEFA wanted to bring footballers together in a continental competition and be influential in discussions at the FIFA World Cup. The Union started with 31 nations and has now grown to 55 members.

The biggest European football competition is the UEFA European Championship (often known as the Euros) which takes place every four years, normally two years away from the FIFA World Cup. Footballers dream of representing their country in the Euros and the tournament results are front page news. In 2021 Italy won the Euros for the second time after first winning in 1968. The UEFA Women's Championship was created in 1984 and takes the same form as the men's competition. The Women's Championship is very hard fought and the title has been won by Germany more times

than all the other teams put together.

The UEFA Champions League has 32 European football teams compete against each other each season. Real Madrid from Spain were the first team to win the Champions League. They have won 13 times in total – that's more than any other team. The UEFA Badge of Honour is stitched onto the uniforms of any club that wins three Champions League titles in a row, or five in total. So far Barcelona, Real Madrid, AC Milan, Bayern Munich, Ajax and Liverpool all have the UEFA Badge of Honour on their kits. The tournament is fast-paced and exciting – the quickest goal ever scored was by Roy Makaay from Bayern Munich who scored against Real Madrid only 11 seconds into the match!

UEFA also funds charitable work all over the world. The UEFA Foundation for Children was established to support humanitarian projects such as health, education and integration. They use football to bring children together to inspire learning, personal development and healthy lifestyles. The Foundation funds projects all over the world through football camps, academies and outreach programmes.

THE ALL BLACKS

New Zealand's national men's rugby team, the All Blacks, are the most successful men's international rugby team ever. They have won more than three quarters of the matches they have played – no other national team has come close to this record. The team is known as the All Blacks because every part of their uniform – their jersey, shorts and socks – is black.

If there's one thing the All Blacks won't tolerate, it's divas – there are no superstars and nobody is bigger than the team. The most important thing is to have a common goal. This comes from the Māori word *whānau*, which means extended family. The All Blacks want to draw on their rich Māori heritage which teaches that the team is more important than the individual. According to this philosophy, you will never succeed on your own, but you will be successful as an individual if the team functions well. The All Blacks are very much a family team – there have been 47 sets of brothers on the team and 19 fathers and sons. They also make sure that they are always looking to the future. They have a youth team

where players under 10 years old are known appropriately as Small Blacks.

The All Blacks perform a haka before each match. A haka is a traditional Māori challenge or posture dance. In the haka, the team chant, stamp their feet and vigorously move in unison. While sometimes used by warriors, the haka is also a ceremonial dance and an important part of Māori culture. The All Blacks have played an important role in introducing this part of Māori culture to a global audience. The focus on Māori heritage comes from the All Black's pride in their native New Zealand.

The Original All Blacks is the name given to the 1905 team, who were the first New Zealand rugby team to tour the world. The Original All Blacks were also the first to wear an all-black uniform and take the name. Their tour of Britain, France and America is legendary – they scored 976 points, only conceding 59. The Original All Blacks were successful because they valued teamwork, communication and cooperation.

VENUS AND SERENA WILLIAMS

Venus and Serena Williams are two sisters who became the greatest tennis players in the world. They changed the sport forever and ushered in a new era of women's tennis. Both Venus and Serena have been ranked number one in the world during their respective careers and for over a decade they dominated the women's game. Venus is the older sister by just over a year and has won 49 singles titles over the course of her career, while Serena has won an amazing 73 singles titles.

Venus and Serena grew up in Lynwood, California, and were coached by their father, Richard Williams, who pushed them hard to become the best. At the time there were very few Black professional tennis players, and even fewer Black female professional tennis players. Richard claimed that he knew that his daughters would be world champions even before they were born. He started teaching Venus tennis when she was four, on a court in East Compton Park in Los Angeles. Later, he moved the family from California to Florida, where Venus and Serena trained at the Delray Beach Tennis academy six hours a day, six days a week

for years. Their hard work soon paid off: by 14, Venus was a professional tennis player and was ranked number one in the world before her 20th birthday. Serena became number one in 2002, taking her sister's title from her. Serena was the world's highest paid female athlete in 2017, earning almost $27 million in prize money and endorsements that year.

One of the reasons the Williams sisters are so incredible is that they had to compete against each other, inspiring them to be better tennis players. Venus won Wimbledon for the second time in 2001 and went on to play Serena in the US Open final. Though Venus took the title, she said at the time, 'I don't exactly feel like I've won. I just hate to see Serena lose, even against me. I'm the big sister. I make sure she has everything, even if I don't have anything. I love her and it's hard.'

The sisters have played each other many times in their careers and have played against each other in professional matches 31 times. Serena has won the majority of these, leading 19 games to 12. Venus and Serena may be strong when

they play against each other, but they are incredible when they team up and play together in doubles matches. They have won 22 doubles titles, including 14 Grand Slams and three Olympic gold medals.

The sisters have changed the world of tennis and their legacy will be felt for years to come. Seeing two Black sisters take on the world and win is a compelling story for any young player. Venus and Serena continue to inspire a new generation with many younger players on the women's tour crediting the sisters for their interest in the sport. The Williams sisters' legacy has also inspired a new generation of tennis players from diverse backgrounds to enter the sport.

SHAKESPEARE'S PLAYERS

William Shakespeare's plays are still performed, studied and loved centuries after his death in 1616. His plays were written for a team of actors, called players. Shakespeare wrote some parts for specific actors because he knew the strengths and weaknesses of his players and the parts that they liked to play. For example, some actors were funnier at clowning around, so Shakespeare wrote the part of Dogberry in *Much Ado About Nothing* for actor William Kemp as it had lots of physical comedy. William Kemp

was a popular comic actor at the time, but he was also known to improvise his lines on stage. Other actors were better with funny speeches, so the part of the fool in *King Lear* was written with many witty lines for actor Robert Armin.

An acting company in Shakespeare's time would have had to work as a team if they wanted to be successful. Young actors would join the company as apprentices and work their way up to larger roles. They wouldn't just have to know how

to deliver lines, actors would need to be able to sword fight, sing, dance and even deal with unruly crowds. There was a lot to learn from the more experienced members.

Shakespeare's acting company was originally called the Lord Chamberlain's Men, later changing its name to King's Men, after James I became king. Shakespeare was a shareholder in the company, which means he shared in the profits (and costs). During Shakespeare's time only men and boys were

allowed to be actors, so boys would play the female roles, with men sometimes playing older women. Just like today, actors were famous and would draw big crowds. Richard Burbage was one of the most famous actors of the time and performed the title role in the first performances of many of Shakespeare's most-famous plays, including *Hamlet*, *Richard III*, *King Lear* and *Othello*. Burbage was so popular that when he died in 1619 the public mourning was almost greater than that for Queen Anne, who had died 10 days earlier.

The plays would also be changed by the theatre that they were performed in while touring the country. Larger, indoor theatres could use more special effects or bigger set pieces, such as those required to create a spectacular masked ball scene in *The Tempest*. The Globe theatre in London is one of the most famous venues for Shakespeare's players.

Unluckily, the theatre burned down in 1613 when a theatrical cannon misfired during a performance of *Henry VIII*. Thankfully, no-one was hurt, although one man had to put out his burning trousers with a bottle of ale! The Globe was rebuilt near its original location in London and opened in 1997 where modern Shakepeare's players perform regularly.

THE BOLSHOI BALLET

One of the most famous ballet companies in the world, the Moscow-based Bolshoi Ballet, has been entertaining audiences with its signature ballet style for nearly 250 years. *Bolshoi* means 'big' or 'grand' in Russian, so the Bolshoi Ballet is literally the 'Big Ballet'. The ballet prides itself on being a symbol of Russian culture and is a link between traditional Russian musical culture and the modern world. It is hugely popular across the globe – even Lady Gaga is a fan!

The company was formed in 1776 by Russian Prince Urusov and English businessman and former acrobat Michael Maddox. At first it was the dance school for the Moscow orphanage, but it soon got its own theatre and premises. As the company grew it took in members from diverse backgrounds, from peasant artists to guest stars from abroad. After the Russian revolution in 1917, Moscow became the capital of the Soviet Union. Soon, the Bolshoi became the biggest ballet company in Soviet

Russia, performing ballets which connected the people with revolutionary themes and characters. The company grew and grew, nurturing new dancers and taking in talent from all over Russia.

When the Bolshoi Ballet first toured the West in 1956, the scale and power of the dancing amazed audiences wherever they performed. The fast and powerful technique used by dancers of the Bolshoi changed the way that ballet

was performed around the world, and the Bolshoi soon became the Soviet Union's most important cultural export. Even today, one of the most important aspects of the Bolshoi Ballet is to promote ballet and Russian culture to the world through touring.

The Bolshoi Ballet is a community where dancers collaborate and help each other. The Moscow Choreographic Institute was set up to help pass down knowledge between generations so that young stars can be individually coached by retired Bolshoi dancers. Dancers train together six days a week for long hours and form very close bonds. Duet classes are a key part of training, where dancers work closely with a partner on routines and lifts, making sure that they can coordinate perfectly.

The Bolshoi Ballet is a huge source of national pride in Russia, bringing people together in their love of dance and tradition. Crowds flock to see feats of technical brilliance and loudly interrupt the ballet performances with their cheers. The Bolshoi Ballet's style is famously colourful, powerful and dynamic. It brings together technique and athleticism, as well as dramatic intensity. Alexander Gorsky, a former dancer and ballet master, believed that acting was as important as dancing, and his teachings have been a cornerstone of the ballet ever since.

CHINESE ACROBATICS

Acrobatic acts and feats of gymnastics have been an important part of Chinese culture for thousands of years. In China, acrobatics was traditionally seen as the art of the working people. It brought people together because it was not a highbrow or exclusive form of entertainment, rather anyone could enjoy it. Chinese acrobatics came from everyday life, with acrobats skilfully using common objects like tables, bowls, chairs and rings for their tricks, as they had to use whatever they had at hand. The first records of acrobatics were seen in the Xia Dynasty, over

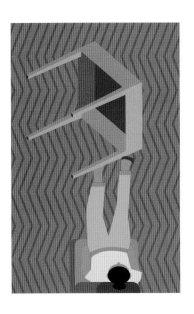

4,000 years ago, and these feats are still popular today. During the Han Dynasty (221-22 AD), acrobatic acts became more evolved, incorporating music and a wider variety of techniques, and became known as 'the show of a hundred tricks'.

Chinese acrobats must study intensively and work very closely with the rest of the troupe. Many tricks require precise, split-second coordination between acrobats in order to work, and can be very dangerous, so the troupe members have to trust each other with their lives. The two key pillars of this form of acrobatics are strength and coordination. Acrobats must be extremely strong in the core and legs to maintain movement and balance, but they also have to be coordinated to maintain harmony with other acrobats.

Chinese acrobatic troupes are an important form of cultural exchange between China and other nations – over 100 Chinese acrobatic troupes tour the world. Chinese acrobatics has seen a resurgence in popularity and today is considered part of the national arts in China. The most popular Chinese acrobatic show in the

UK is the Chinese State Circus, which first started touring in the 1990s.

There are two main styles of Chinese acrobatics; martial arts style acrobatics, which tend to emphasise fighting scenes and often use weapons, and circus style acrobatics, which are closer to Western acrobatic shows with performers, acrobatics, jugglers and gymnasts.

There are many traditional acrobatic acts. The Lion dance is a feat where acrobats combine to imitate the strength and agility of a lion, while Wushu is a traditional form of group gymnastics, complete with somersaults, kicking, jumping and pulling poses. Some acrobats perform on high wires or on fixed poles, while juggling and tumbling are also popular.

Modern Chinese acrobats have incorporated elements such as bicycles, lights and trapezes, while still using traditional acrobatic skills. Popular stories are often used as a framework for acrobatic feats, such as the Monkey King, which is a popular traditional tale about a character who can practice magic and turn into different animals.

CULTURE
STONEHENGE

One of the world's oldest and most famous monuments, Stonehenge dates back over 5,000 years. The giant stones can be seen from miles around, but nobody knows what they were gathered for and who put them there. There are many things we still don't know about Stonehenge, but we do know that it took many people hundreds of years to build. Building of Stonehenge began around 3,000 BC and it is estimated the last changes were made in the early Bronze Age, around 1,500 BC.

Two types of stones were used to build Stonehenge; larger, rock-like sarsen stones and smaller bluestones. Stonehenge stands on Salisbury Plain, in Wiltshire, UK and some of the bluestones were transported over 180 miles from Pembrokeshire in west Wales. This is very unusual because most stone monuments at that time were constructed using stone from no more than 10 miles away. Bluestones were chiselled from the rock face, then transported on wooden sledges using log rollers. Workers used ropes,

wooden wedges, mallets and levers and had to work closely together to transport these massive stones over such a long distance. These stones were incredibly heavy – the smaller bluestones weigh about 3,600 kg (8,000 lb), which is as much as two cars, while the heavier sarsen stones weigh the same as a lorry!

There are many different theories about why ancient Britons built Stonehenge and what they used it for. Some think that the stone circle is designed

to study the movements of the Sun and the Moon, as ancient Britons believed in their magical properties and thought they had special powers. Every year, on 21st June (the Summer Solstice and longest day of the year) the Sun rises directly over a stone called the Heel Stone. Perhaps Stonehenge was used as a sort of calendar, with ceremonies held on the longest and shortest days of the year. Every year people gather at Stonehenge to watch the sun rise for the Summer Solstice.

Another theory is that Stonehenge was a primitive computer, designed to calculate the movement of the Sun and Moon. Others think that Stonehenge was a place of healing and a spiritual centre for ancient Britain. We do know that it was used as a cemetery, as over 200 people have been found buried on the grounds.

There are other giant, man-made circles similar to Stonehenge. One of them, Woodhenge, is only two miles from Stonehenge, and was built around 2,500 BC. It is believed to have had a different purpose than Stonehenge and doesn't seem to have been quite so sacred, as abandoned tools and building materials have been discovered there.

Despite all the mysteries surrounding Stonehenge, we do know that it is a masterpiece of human ingenuity and teamwork, and must have required huge effort from hundreds of well-organised people.

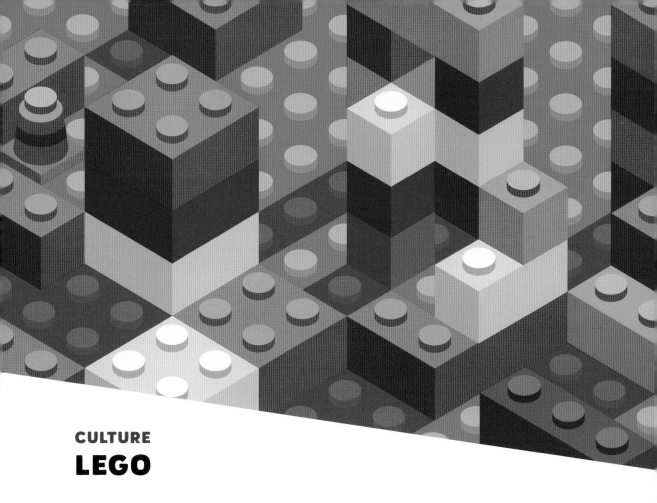

LEGO

Ranked as the 'world's most powerful brand' in 2015, the LEGO company was founded in 1934 by Danish toymaker Ole Kirk Christiansen and originally made wooden toys. Christiansen was famous for demanding perfection, saying, 'only the best is good enough'. The word LEGO comes from two Danish words *leg* and *godt*, meaning 'play well'. The word *Lego* in Latin also means 'I put together'.

The interlocking LEGO brick wasn't launched until 1958 but is now a worldwide symbol of play. The design of the brick means that different bricks can be put together no matter which set they come from and new bricks made today can fit with old bricks made years ago.

LEGO is not just important for play. Some social and development centres use LEGO bricks to help children develop teamwork and social skills. Working collaboratively in a small group to create something together helps children with communication, creativity and confidence. LEGO bricks also help build fine motor skills, as well as focus, concentration and patience.

There are ten LEGOLAND amusement parks across Denmark, the UK, Germany, Malaysia, the US, Japan and the United Arab Emirates. As well as rides and rollercoasters, the parks are designed to contain educational elements for younger visitors. There are also hundreds of LEGO events

all over the world every year, where LEGO fans meet up to discuss LEGO and show off their latest builds. These events attract thousands of people and the LEGO creations on display range from traditional sets to complete cities. The largest LEGO sculpture ever created is a 13-metre-high (42 ft) version of London's Tower Bridge. The bridge took 5,805,846 pieces of LEGO to create and is the holder of a Guinness World Record for largest LEGO sculpture (most bricks). The bridge is big enough and strong enough that several cars can drive over it at the same time.

LEGO is so popular that it is literally out of this world. In 2011 the Space Shuttle *Endeavour* took LEGO sets to the International Space Station so scientists could study how the bricks would react to the lack of gravity in space. Later that same year, NASA launched the *Juno* Spacecraft, which is an unmanned craft destined for the planet Jupiter. Aboard that craft were three LEGO minifigures – the Roman god Jupiter, his wife Juno and the astronomer Galileo.

CULTURE
ABBA

ABBA are Sweden's biggest pop group and one of the most successful and popular music groups of all time. They have sold over 150 million records worldwide and had eight number one albums in a row. The group takes its name from the first letter of the first name of the four members, Agnetha, Benny, Björn and Anni-Frid. For a while ABBA consisted of two married couples; band members Agnetha Fältskog and Björn Ulvaeus were married, as were Benny Anderssen and Anni-Frid Lyngstad. All four members were talented musicians before they met, but it wasn't until they started working together that they were able to create music that changed the world.

Benny, Bjorn, Anni-Frid and Agnetha liked how their voices sounded together, and there was obviously a great chemistry between the band members as they wrote their first song within a few weeks of forming. Benny and Bjorn wrote many of ABBA's early hits in a small office in Stockholm, and at first would ask their manager Stig Anderson for help writing lyrics in English. They knew that only Agnetha and Anni-Frid could give the songs the depth and emotion that they needed.

ABBA won the Eurovision Song Contest in 1974 with the song 'Waterloo', which is still popular to this day. As part of the 50th anniversary celebrations for the Eurovision Song Contest, 'Waterloo' was voted the best song in the history of the contest. The band had a huge run of worldwide hits, including 'Dancing Queen', 'SOS', 'Mamma Mia' and 'Knowing Me, Knowing You'.

A musical based on ABBA's songs called *Mamma Mia!* was first shown in London in 1999 and has since been performed in 50 countries. It was the ninth longest-running Broadway show in New York, running for 14 years. The musical has been adapted into two movies, *Mamma Mia!* and its sequel *Mamma Mia! Here We Go Again*, which have made nearly a billion dollars in worldwide box office takings. There's even *Mamma Mia! The Party*, a dinner theatre show, where fans of ABBA come together to eat, dance and see their favourite songs performed live.

There is an ABBA museum in their home city of Stockholm, where fans can gather to share their love of ABBA. It contains a piano that is electronically linked to Benny's own piano in his home, so that when he plays at home, so does the piano in the museum.

ABBA split in 1982 but their music has continued to bring people together for decades. The band reformed in 2021, celebrating with a new album and a tour, where their songs are performed by hologramatic avatars, or, as they call them, ABBA-tars.

BTS

BTS have broken many records on their way to becoming one of the most popular groups in the world. They have sold millions of albums and are the first South Korean band to have number one singles in the US and the UK. BTS are a K-pop (or Korean pop) group made up of seven members, Jin, Suga, J-Hope, RM, Jimin, V and Jungkook. BTS is an acronym for *Bangtan Sonyeondan*, which roughly translates as 'Bulletproof Boy Scouts', and they also call themselves the Bangtan Boys. BTS emphasise the importance of kindness, inclusivity and empathy, and they are a band who want to bring people together.

One of the reasons that the band is so popular is the subject of their music. Other bands sing about relationships and love, but BTS songs are often about things like bullying, mental health, loss and other troubles that their fans might encounter. Talking about these issues can help their fans make sense of the world and their feelings. One of the themes of their music is that we can become better people through sharing experiences and music.

The band works together to create dance routines for their songs, sometimes working 12 to 15 hour days to make sure that they are completely in sync with each other. Despite becoming so popular very

quickly, the band say that BTS is a democracy, with RM once claiming that group decisions are settled by a round of rock-paper-scissors. They spend a lot of time together, even when they are not working, and feel the close-knit community of a family.

Another important ingredient to BTS's success is their devoted fans, who have come together to help build the band's success. BTS fans call themselves the ARMY, which stands for 'Adorable Representative M.C. For Youth', and have over 40 million members worldwide. BTS broke the record for the most YouTube views in 24 hours when the video for their song 'Dynamite' reached 101.1 million views in one day. Their worldwide fans are passionate advocates for BTS and over one million fans from around the world watched a live stream concert in October 2020.

In 2017 BTS started working with UNICEF on the Love Myself anti-violence campaign. As well as promoting messages to prevent violence, the band has donated a portion of the profits from album sales to UNICEF Korea. The campaign has raised over $3 million globally with the money supporting young victims of violence. This message of anti-violence is a theme in many BTS songs and is part of the band's legacy.

TOGETHER WE CAN!

Most living things on planet Earth work together in some way, from birds cleaning the teeth of hippos, to clownfish working with sea anemones to protect their eggs. Mankind isn't unique in working as a team, but we are able to do it on a much larger scale than any other animal.

Teamwork makes us happier, improves our lives and helps us grow. We need different perspectives and voices to help us understand the world and our place in it. The best way for us to grow, learn and discover who we are is as part of a team. The examples of brilliant achievements in this book don't just help mankind, they have helped all the people who have been involved in them.

Great ideas don't often come from lone geniuses working on their own – most of the time they come from teams bouncing ideas off each other and refining concepts. Every single great technological, cultural and artistic leap has happened when people have come together. We have put a man on the Moon and we've fought global pandemics, and the only way that we were able to do that was by recruiting thousands of people to work together for a common purpose.

The next century will present us with huge challenges including inequality, climate change and global health, and the only way that we will be able to meet these challenges is by working together. The examples in this book show that there's nothing we can't accomplish with the right team.

The book that you are holding in your hands wouldn't exist without people working together for a common purpose. This one book involved a writer, editor, illustrator, designer, proofreader, and teams in production, sales, marketing and publicity. Then many people at the printer made the physical book, which was then transported to different countries and delivered to bookshops to be sold. Together, as part of a team, we got this book to you.

We hope you liked it.

NED HARTLEY

Ned Hartley is a writer and editor of many books for children, including *Spider-Man: An Origin*, *Marvel Museum*, *The Ladybird Big Book of Dead Things*, *Albert Einstein: A Graphic History*, *Paperscapes: The Jungle Book* and a small fleet of *Star Wars* annuals. Ned also writes *Bananaman* for the *Beano* comic every week and *The Steel Commando* for *Monster Fun* comic. He lives in London with his wife and his greatest collaboration: their two children.

STUDIO MUTI

Studio Muti is a creative studio based in Cape Town, South Africa. They are a dedicated team of illustrators and designers who are passionate about producing original and inspiring artwork. Studio Muti have illustrated many books including, *Infographics: Technology*, *Amazing Treasures: 100+ Objects and Places That Will Boggle Your Mind* and *Harry Potter: Exploring Diagon Alley* among others.